A Reality Guide for Cheating Women and Men

MEN SPEAK THE TRUTH:
About Why They Cheat

Listen To Your Man,
Save Your Friendship
Save Your Relationship
Save Your Family
Save Your Marriage
Keep Your Man...

by
Sylvia Beach

Men Speak The Truth: About Why They Cheat

Copyright ©2019 by Sylvia Beach

All rights reserved. No part of this publication may be reproduced, scanned, stored in a retrieval system, or transmitted in any form or by any means without the prior written permission of the publisher, nor be otherwise circulated in any form of binding or cover other than that in which it is published and without a similar condition being imposed on the subsequent purchaser. Please do not participate in or encourage piracy of copyrighted materials in violations of the author's rights. Purchase only authorized editions.

ISBN: 9781071184752

Women Need to Know What Men are Saying
Men Speak the Truth: About Why They Cheat

A GUIDE FOR WOMEN

MEN TELL YOU ABOUT WHAT THEY NEED AND WHY THEY CHEAT

The purpose of my book is to inspire and help strengthen relationships

1 Corinthians 13:4–8a
Love is patient, love is kind. It does not envy, it does not boast, it is not proud. It is not rude, it is not self-seeking, it is not easily angered, and it keeps no record of wrongs. Love does not delight in evil but rejoices with the truth. It always protects, always trusts, always hopes, and always perseveres.
Love never fails.

To StarShinna Beach
The Love of my Life

To my loving parents
Stella and James

To all the women and men in the world who are in love and looking for love.

About the Author

Sylvia Beach is a single mother to her daughter StarShinna Beach. Sylvia was born and raised on the eastern shore of Virginia. She attended Hare Valley Elementary School in Northampton County. Her parents moved to Painter, Virginia where she attended middle and high school in Accomack County. In 1982, she graduated from Central High School in Painter, Virginia.

Sylvia attended Virginia State University in 1994 majoring in Elementary Education. She moved back home to pursue a career as a receptionist from the Eastern Shore Community College. She received an associate degree while working as a receptionist for Accomack County Parks and Recreation.

In 2002, she and her daughter moved to Maryland for a career change. During that time, she received her bachelor and master's degrees from American InterContinental University in Business Administration-Human Resource Management, graduating with honors.

As a teenager, Sylvia found a passion for lingerie. She

never gave up on her lingerie dreams. In her master's program, she created her future lingerie business plan. In 2005, one day after work, Sylvia sat on the side of her bed and began to draw and label part of her designs. She knew she was not an artist and therefore her lingerie designs came from God; whom she gives all the credit. Her daughter had a friend "Travis" in school who was gifted in art. He could draw murals by hand. After discovering this, she asked Travis to beautify her lingerie drawings, and so he did. She held onto her designs for years until she felt she was financially prepared to expedite her God-given products in the name of "Sylvia's Lingerie Collection."

About the Book and My Life Experience

*M*y book is to enlighten women to what men are delivering and how to appreciate and maintain what you presently have. My book talks about marriage, love, commitment and how to keep it from going wrong.

My book is for all readers; young ladies, young men, and especially for those who are married or in committed relationships.

Find out how love turns into a pain within the blink of an eye. We think we know, but better yet…let's find out from the men who know best.

Men tell us why men cheat. Cheating is viewed by people as a bad act. How bad is cheating? How did it get to a cheating point and how can women avoid the pain of a cheating partner?

There are many reasons why cheating occurs, whether it's the woman or the man who is cheating. After reading this book, my prayer is that you can consume the messages and apply them to your life and relationship.

I will start by informing you of how and why I decided to express and provide my message.

Living a single life isn't all that bad; there were struggles for me and my daughter along the way, but I found ways to make it. Raising a daughter; working full and part-time jobs while earning degrees was tough, but I still found time to have a social life. I met some wonderful male friends along the way. I did what I had to do to survive, but I did it respectfully and privately. I knew it was wrong, but I felt as though I wasn't hurting the unknown.

Throughout my life, I didn't go looking for sex. I looked for love. Looking for love wasn't bringing me what I wanted, which was my own man. It would always bring me someone else's man. There were those I didn't want to be bothered with, and there were those that I found interest in and enjoyed the moments with. Those who were in a committed relationship made it wrong, but yet it felt so right. I felt loved and secure, but most of all I had someone who spent quality time with me. My daughter and I were always loved and taken care of, wanting for much of nothing.

I'm not ashamed of what I did because I protected the unknown if you will. I didn't hurt or intentionally hurt anyone. As years passed, I was getting tired of picking up another woman's slack. I would ask but still never could understand why. There came a part of my life when I woke up to discover that being a part-time lover is hard and was getting old, but I didn't stop.

I met a man and put my life on hold for him because I felt he was my soul mate. I continued the relationship because I was happy. There were times I wanted to leave but being in love with him hindered me. It was wrong, but I couldn't leave for many reasons including love. I didn't get the benefits that his partner was receiving; which for me was the difficult part of it all. Through it all, I felt fulfilled and looked forward to the surprises and even the little things that meant so much to me just because they were from him. I was spoiled with treasures that no one else provided to or for me. Having him and those benefits were my dream that never came true. I now know what quality, luxury, and life are about and most of all, I now know myself. Thanks to him, I set my bar high but never too high for my God-sent future husband.

Each time I met a man it was a long-term relationship which made me feel as if I had my own man until the holidays came. The emptiness and loneliness weren't fun. During the emptiness and loneliness periods, I would personally pretend I was in a long distance relationship; even when he was only 20 to 30 minutes away from me. Pretending this would dry my tears until we connected again whether it was by phone or in person. I would say to myself and pretend that it was the same as a long-distance relationship only to get me by until we could be together again.

I was in love for 11 years and hoped that we could be together forever, but I was only kidding myself. We separated for some time, and that is when I was able to distinguish what love and being in love was. We loved each other, but I was in love. He wasn't in love with me because I'm still single. I don't feel that I wasted time in my life because it was all worth it and it paid off. I realized that men in commitments are going to and will hunt for what they are seeking or longing for; but also, that the committed partner has more control over the relationship than he realizes unless she doesn't care.

While dating men, I would ask each, "Why are you here with me instead of being with your partner?" It was funny how I received the same answers.

A sample of their responses includes these: "She doesn't want to give me sex," "I can't touch her," "She isn't as sexually active as you," "We don't have a relationship anymore," "I'm not loved at home, and you show me more love than she ever has," "She doesn't know what to do, she just lay there," and "I'd just rather be here with you."

There are even more reasons they shared with me such as, she is always tired, she doesn't feel like it, or she has a headache, etc.

I want to share something with the ladies; if you aren't submissive and you don't provide your man with intimacy, sex, and love, someone is waiting to fill your shoes.

If this isn't a concern of yours, or you don't care what men are saying; I recommend you let that man go. My reason is that you probably care about his well-being and not his actual feelings. Not caring for someone you say you love might work if he is your friend or a friend with benefits. If he is your partner, love will make you care, and being in love will make you complete.

Listen, there is a shortage of men and an abundance of women who are looking and waiting for a good man. I'm here to share with you ways to keep your man happy.

I'm still waiting for God to send me MY OWN MAN; so, on that note…thank God you have one.

Read my book to see what men's expectations are of a woman.

Table of Contents

About the Author I

About the Book and My Life Experience III

What is CHEATING? 1

The Unthinkable True Love Affair 3

Identifying the Signs of a CHEATING Man… 9

What a Man Needs in a RELATIONSHIP 17

My Opinion on the 90-Day Rule 29

The 80/20 Rule in a Relationship 35

For the Love of Money and for the Love of Fame 39

The Dos in a Relationship… 43

The Don'ts in a Relationship… 49

What Does it Take to Save Your Relationship? 55

How to Determine When it's Time to Depart? 63

Did You Give Up Without a Fight? 69

Why Men Say They Cheat? 81

Why Does it Hurt so Bad? 91

Test Your Relationship, Take this Survey 99

Acknowledgments 103

CHAPTER 1
What is CHEATING?

Cheating is an action taken in deceit, fraud or trickery:

Breaking the rules. This is when you don't care; ignoring what you and your partner agreed.

You are being misled. This is when you use very poor judgment.

Cheating is being unfaithful. This is when you break a promise to be loyal and exclusive.

You are committing adultery. This is when you engage in a sexual act with someone other than your husband or wife.

To trick another. This is when you use someone else for your gain.

When one is untrustworthy. Means you can't be trusted, not reliable or dependable.

An act of selfishness. This is when one doesn't care about anyone but themselves. It's all about self. Me, myself and I (Me, me, me; my, my, my; I, I, I). A relationship cannot be one-sided. If this is you, then your relationship has already failed. It takes two in partnership to succeed. Being selfish will cause your partner to seek fulfillment elsewhere.

You are showing disrespect to another. OMG, when you disrespect another, there is only one reason. That is, you don't have any respect for yourself. To show rudeness and anger are actual signs of unhappiness and a bad attitude. If this is often demonstrated in a relationship, think twice about a long-term commitment.

REMEMBER: You cannot change a person; they have to change him or herself.

CHAPTER 2

The Unthinkable True Love Affair

Wikipedia states a romance is an emotional feeling of love for, or a strong attraction towards, another person, and the courtship behaviors undertaken by an individual to express those overall feelings and resultant emotions. Although the emotions and sensations of romantic love are widely associated with sexual attraction, romantic feelings can exist without expectation of physical consummation and be subsequently expressed.

Atlantis and Sonny

Atlantis was a young lady who was single with a son. They lived from paycheck to paycheck. One day, Atlantis was working providing her daily routine duties. She met this man named Sonny. Sonny had no shame in letting her know he admired her. He complimented her on her attire and hair, giving her the nickname "Ponytail."

Every week it was as if he waited to see her coming to appear in her path to greet her with some admiration. On one particular workday, Sonny appeared in Atlantis's office to make a payment. She greeted him and handed him his receipt. He left, and she realized he overpaid her. She ran him down to inform and give his money back. He gazed into her eyes and said keep it for your lunch, but Atlantis insisted that he take his money, as he refused.

A few weeks went by, and once again, as Atlantis went to the post office, Sonny showed up. This particular day he built his nerves up enough to start a conversation by making flattering remarks, which would make any woman smile. He then asked if he could call her sometime. She paused with doubt and uncertainty, but said yes, even surprising herself. The next day, Sonny called her office, and the conversation was enjoyable and well-received by Atlantis. After the warm and engaging conversation, Sonny asked Atlantis for her phone number. She was then more than delighted to give it to him.

Their communication of getting to know each other emerged into a special friendship. The late-night phone calls of laughter, sharing life experiences and his compliments and appreciations of her being a single mother were sweet music to her ears.

One night, he revealed he was a married man and how his marriage evolved. Atlantis listened, and it didn't interfere with their new friendship at all. As time passed and their friendship grew, Sonny wanted to treat her with surprises and gifts because he felt Atlantis was a hard-working single mother who deserved beautiful things.

Sonny knew Atlantis was a sophisticated, fashionable woman; so, one day he mentioned that Hecht's Department Store was having a big sale and he wanted her to buy a few outfits for herself at his expense. She was overwhelmed and didn't want any strings to be attached to his cost. On the other hand, no one has ever offered her such a gift. She took Sonny up on his offer, and from that day the gifts, surprises, groceries and total respect never stopped. Sonny even went as far as to introduce his elderly mother, which was such a loving moment to Atlantis.

Sonny's mother's attachment was so bonding; it became as if Atlantis was her daughter-in-law. The friendship was accepted by his mother which then opened the door of trust. Sonny began to reveal the problematic family issues he was experiencing. After hearing the mistreatment he was suffering from his wife and son, Atlantis found herself heartbroken. Sonny said he would prefer to spend money on someone who deserves it and appreciates it. He continued to provide Atlantis with food, clothes, birthday parties, cash for household bills, jewelry, etc.

Atlantis new lifestyle was her dream come true. The only thing she was missing was the intimacy. She was content with their friendship, but Sonny wanted more. Their age difference had Sonny frightened to engage with Atlantis sexually. So, he kept it the way it was the "Unthinkable True Love Affair."

Atlantis had a job offer which relocated her. She had to

break the news to Sonny. When she did, he was happy and excited for her. Later, the truth be told; he was very heartbroken knowing that the one who gave him his life back is no longer going to be around. Sonny never stopped being supportive and encouraged her to pursue her dreams.

One Sunday morning, Atlantis met Sonny. He decided to expose his true feelings to her. He said he spoke with his friends about the young woman he was in love with relocating to another state. His friends told him to follow his heart and go with her. Once Sonny opened up, Atlantis being the loving, caring and sensitive woman who was raised to do the right things from the heart asked Sonny to relocate with her and her son. Out of respect and fear, he felt his age would hold Atlantis back in life. Atlantis insisted stating she would take care of him, but Sonny did not accept the offer. Two weeks later Atlantis accepted the job offer and relocated with her son.

Over some time, things changed. Sonny no longer provided assistance and luxuries. Life was difficult, and the distance decreased the conversations. Atlantis saw Sonny a few times after that but then a few years went by, and life moved on. Atlantis would still think about Sonny but had no way of contacting him or seeing him.

One afternoon, Atlantis received a phone call that devastated her. She learned that Sonny had passed away. Never in her life did she see or knew what was coming after his death.

Atlantis never knew how much she loved Sonny until she received the phone call. Atlantis went into a state of depression with no one to turn to. The unstoppable tears, not being able to work, no desire to see sunlight, no strength to get out of bed, the guilt of not saying good-bye and wondering why this was happening to her was shocking.

One morning, God spoke to Atlantis telling her to turn on the television. Atlantis turned on the TV, and a man was teaching about death and the stages one goes through during a time of death. When Atlantis discovered the category she fell in, she knew then that there are so many others in a worse place than she. At that point, she regained herself, she prayed to God with confidence that her life will emerge, and so it did.

Although Sonny was in a better place, Atlantis will forever be grateful for him. Atlantis never knew or thought that she loved Sonny until he died. This was the Unthinkable True Love Affair.

CHAPTER 3

Identifying the Signs of a CHEATING Man...

Changes in their behavior or activity pattern. Many men have a routine, such as working from 9 to 5, now he is working to 7 or 8 o'clock. Maybe he is a family man who stays home, and suddenly he goes to visit his friends more often. More time is spent away from home than at home.

Excuses for not wanting sex. When men get caught up and enjoy outside sex, they don't want to have sex at home because it's not as enjoyable.

New sex positions. Men experience a new position they really enjoy and want to share it with their partner at home.

Starting arguments or fights. Men need to find a way to get to their lover; one of the most common ways is to start an argument to leave home.

Wedding band removal. A man who displays to be single by removing his wedding ring to capture women.

They are secretive. A faithful man has no secrets. A husband and wife should never have secrets. If he suddenly has passwords on the computer or cell phone, wants a separate savings account, wants his privacy in the bathroom, or spends time alone in the house with his cell phone, these are signs of an affair.

Change in attitude. If your man has a not-interested attitude and never wants to be bothered. If he no longer wants to talk or play and is just serious all the time, there is a disconnect in the relationship.

Additional travel. All of a sudden, his trips are more frequent without notification or explanation. You not being invited to travel with him is a sign that he wants to spend more time with his mistress.

He wants to know where you are regularly. A man wants to know where you are so that he will know what moves he can make and how much time he has to spend with his mistress.

Deleted cell phone numbers. Removing cell numbers is a sign he doesn't want you to know or see a particular name, so there are no connections to his mistress.

He leaves the room when talking on his cell. A man not wanting to take calls in front of you is a clue that he does not want you to know who he is talking to.

The smell of a woman's fragrance. A woman's perfume is personal and preference. If you smell a scent and it isn't in your collection; that is a sign of cheating. Even if he tries to cover up by drinking alcohol, it doesn't remove a perfume smell so don't be fooled by his twist of stating it is your perfume. On the other hand, this may not be a sure sign of cheating, but it is a sign that a woman touched him to get her scent on him.

He is improving his appearance. He changes his appearances in grooming, buying new clothes to dress more professional, keeping his hair cut regularly, wearing new cologne and just looking like a new man.

He has condoms on hand. If a man is married and uses condoms with his wife, he does not need to carry a condom with him. His condoms should be kept at home. If he has a condom on hand, he has intentions to use it outside of the relationship to protect the wife at home.

Sweeter to you than usual. This could be because when he does something nice, it is a ticket out of the house. He could be on a guilt trip knowing he is cheating and taking your trust for granted and wants to assuage his guilty conscience.

Doesn't kiss and touch you the same way he usually does. No two women are the same. Long term infidelity causes adaptation. Example: If you and your husband lip kiss and his mistress French kisses, he will eventually stick his tongue in your mouth by accident.

Comes home refreshed after being out. This is a sign of him being at someone's house or a hotel. It's uncommon that you go out to a club and come home fresher than you were when leaving the house.

Baby, I love you, but I'm not in love with you. This is a turning point in the relationship. He is more into her than he is into you. His feelings and emotions have changed from you to her. This is a sign that someone else is in place.

You have a gut feeling. When you see that things are just different because you know the ins and outs and his patterns and habits. You took notice of things but disregarded them, now there are even more noticeable actions, and you put the pieces together. If your gut feeling indicates, there is another woman, 9 out of 10 times it is.

Just stops saying, "I love you." Men like to secure their woman to ensure she doesn't think negatively about their relationship. Saying I love you is most often exchanged to secure the relationship. When those three words are no longer exchanged it is a sign that if he isn't saying it to you, he is saying it to someone else.

His boys come first. He usually is home, but suddenly he is spending time with the boys. They have weekend activities planned. This gets him out of the house to be with his girl.

Bizarre phone calls and hang-ups. This is a sign that his mistress wants to talk to him. If this takes place and he leaves the room with his phone. He is calling her to ensure she is okay or needs anything.

During arguments, threatening to leave you is an indication that there is somewhere else available to occupy their time. Also, during an argument, a name may be mentioned and talked about.

They usually refer to them as a co-worker who works on their team. Discussing the individual's business only to distract you from putting two and two together.

Catching him in multiple lies. Once he starts telling lies, he will have to continue, but eventually, he will forget what lies he said.

Leaves home in one outfit and comes back in another. Changing clothes or shirts is a red flag that he has been somewhere other than work.

He wants to pay the bills, especially the phone bill. He wants to pay the bills because he has misused money, made long-distance calls and wants to hide the evidence that he is cheating. The phone bill will display the number of requests, the length of time, etc.

They want to experience Viagra. This is when men know they are coming up short in bedroom performance and want their mistress to think they can hold their own; while the wife at home knows that he lacks performance in bed. Now that he has someone new, he is aiming to please by using Viagra.

Wanting additional space. When he wants extra space, it is obvious something, or someone, new has entered that requires time and attention. Take notice of how often and how much spare time he is requesting.

When you want to see his cell phone, he grabs it and becomes defensive. When he grabs his cell, he has something or someone's name he doesn't want you to see. He becomes defensive asking you to respect his privacy.

Unexpected hotel confirmation phone calls. Some hotels will call the given number for confirmation. If the home number is provided that is where the call will go.

Hiding receipts from restaurants, hotels or bills. Cheating is costly and requires confidences. Having unexplained bills mailed to a private mailbox. Purchasing a prepaid credit card to use in buying gifts, paying for hotels and restaurant bills.

Visits internet porn sites. This is a sign that he is interested in other women. Whether it is to fantasize or outside satisfaction it is still a sign of cheating. If the man is on porn sites, he is getting free satisfaction and has replaced the real home sex with internet sex.

He accuses you of cheating. A guilty conscience is a terrible thing when cheating. I love this one because this is an easy one. If the woman knows she isn't cheating and he accuses her, it's because it's vice versa… he is cheating and can't trust himself. Therefore, he doesn't trust you. Any little sign shown; he assumes you are cheating like him.

Twist the question and put it back on you. This is denial, he doesn't want to be questioned or have to answer your questions; therefore, he refers the question back on you. Example: You ask him where were you last night? He responds that he was out with the boys, or asks what did you do last night? Or he asks why you didn't call him if you wanted to know where he was. See how this is put back on you as if you had not a reason to suspect or question him.

His friends act funny towards you. Men don't like drama, especially if they know you. They don't want to have to choose sides when the cheating is exposed. Friends play the innocent role.

Comes home with body marks such as hickies, scratches or abrasions left after intimacy. These are signs of insecurity, disrespect, and cheating. Anytime a mark is placed on a married person; it's because they want the spouse to know what is going on and someone else is sharing their territory.

Female accessories found in the vehicle. If he isn't cheating, did he tell you he gave a female a ride? If not, he is keeping secrets, and she could very well be his mistress.

Lipstick on his collar. If it's not your color or you didn't put it there, he is cheating.

He wants you to change your hairstyle and how you dress. He is now comparing you to his mistress wanting you to change your appearances for him.

CHAPTER 4

What a Man Needs in a RELATIONSHIP

Well…one may say, "It depends on the relationship." My opinion is that all relationships should consist of the basics. Ladies, the basics are the same things that a woman wants; maybe on a different level of standards.

LOVE: Everyone wants to give and receive love. When you are loved, you are appreciated, and someone has your best interest in mind. Let's not get it twisted.

There are two types of love: (1) **Love and (2) Being in love.**

BEING IN LOVE: This type of love is unconditional. It starts excellent; you smile every day, have a boost of energy, share dreams about the future, and have lots of quality time and sex. You start losing weight and dressing with more style, and you are more friendly and more talkative to others. You are feeling good about life in general.

When we are in love, many things change. Hell, our entire lives change. Once we start getting the good stuff, here comes Part 2. We begin to think different, become insecure, scared, and sleepless when that first night comes and you are alone. We get attached, then start questioning who, what, when, and where. Jealousy kicks in; emotions become uncontrollable, curiosity and distrust are out of whack. You begin to see and hear things that are not there. You start to accuse your mate, and you become outraged because what you are thinking, you genuinely do believe. Then you question yourself if this person is the right one.

Yes, it's true. Women are more sensitive and emotional than men. Once our emotions are identified and touched, we become very defensive. Good or bad, the feelings change the behavior and mood which will determine how the day or night will be.

On any given day, a woman could be having a bad day, and her emotions are going crazy. This is when a man should make a phone call to avoid physical contact. The saying goes, "Time and distance heal all wounds."

If you are in a marriage and true love is still there, the two adults must talk about the situation and if it doesn't work at the beginning of the conversation, then end the conversation and give it a day or two. If the two of you are in love, you will know because the friendship and understanding of needing space will take place.

Men say as soon as a woman gets mad, the first thing she does is withhold sex. Well, ladies, truth be told, your "cookie" is a GOD given body part to share with a man.

Genesis 2:18: *And the LORD God said, it is not good that the man should be alone; I will make him a helper suitable for him.*

When you withhold your booty/coochy/cookie/goodies or vajayjay… this is what you are physically saying to the man. "You pissed me off so you can't have any, tonight." Well, I'm here to tell you, just in case you don't know, if you don't have sex with your man, someone else will. Men have needs just like you do. In a committed relationship or marriage; it is the woman's duty to let her man pleasure the coochy.

Let's not forget; men retaliate in a big way. Why??? Because when a woman wants sex, she wants it. When a man says NO, Oh My GOD, here comes war. Ladies, there is no need for war; just remember that you said no. The war began when you withheld the coochy, remember that. Don't accuse or throw out accusations, just roll with it and remember the next time your man wants to spend some good quality time with you and provide some good sex. As the old saying goes: "You reap what you sow."

I feel a woman should be submissive to her man; especially if they are married. I believe there is only one time of each month a man is to leave a woman alone, and that is during her menstruation if she has one. A woman's body goes through a cleansing process which should take its course.

After that, ladies free your pains, the headaches,

backaches, and stomach aches. Making love during those times can be a cure if your man is gentle and respects your aches. Try it, and I guarantee you will love it.

I distributed a survey to over 75 men regardless of race, gender, religion, age, disability, and marital status by asking the question: *"What does a man need in a relationship?"*

I want to share some treasurable information that will help inspire, enlighten and save most relationships beginning with unconditional love.

Unconditional Love – Provide love at respectful limits. We all have GOD given senses, so don't do something to cause harm to yourself.

A Friend – A friend is what you become before you become lovers. This is the beginning of a relationship while building trust. Support your friend in a time of need.

A Partner – Someone who will stand by you right or wrong. Always feel the need to discuss any topic you choose and provide any input, even if the man is wrong. Just because you supported him doesn't mean you can't let him know when the two of you are together and away from others, that he was wrong and why. Remember ladies; a man wants a partner. He isn't looking for a roommate. If he is, he'll tell you he is looking for someone with benefits, and if that is stated in a relationship, run and don't look back.

Affection – This is when you have a feeling of affection or show emotions of caring, being passionate and friendly with him.

Communication – Communication is the key to a successful relationship. Don't expect a man to read your mind. It's not happening. Tell him what you are thinking and explain why. Tell him how much you care about him. Sharing your thoughts and feelings is okay.

Initiative Sex – Be the first to initiate interest in sex. Take action show some love and affection. Be powerful and controlling but make it very enjoyable. The last place to be tired is in bed. No one is competing but know that competition is out there waiting. If you had what it took to get him, then do what it takes to keep him.

Accepted – Hey, you like what you got. If he is workable, then accept him for who he is. Make the man feel wanted and needed. If you can't accept him, then let him go. There is someone for everyone. Free yourself and free the man.

Respect – This is a big one. To respect is to give and receive. To get respect, you must give respect. Most of all, have respect for yourself. Save the disrespect for a private time; smile and play the game. Once the two of you are alone, then it's time to communicate. Explain and discuss what happened and how to avoid it in the future. Ladies, you get much credit when you are a lady and have respect for yourself. Even if you are steaming, keep your cool until it's time to talk it out. Even then, show him that you are a respectful lady.

Trust – First and foremost, you must trust yourself before you can trust someone else. I've heard many times from women, "I love him, so I trust him." Hell, I love most people, but do I trust them? NO. Trust is something you earn, and it takes time to get to know a person. Saying you trust someone is a statement. The question is: "Do you mean it wholeheartedly?"

Ask yourself, is this a person I can depend on for anything? Is this a person I can trust with my life? Is this a person I'm committed to regardless? Is this a person I can tell the truth to whether it's good, bad, or ugly, and accept the consequences? If you answered yes, you are ready to trust and understand what it takes.

Commitment – When you make a commitment, it means both partners are in agreement. This is when both agree to love, respect, be loyal, be honest, trust and be faithful to each other. Even engagement takes place to claim each other and become partners. Know that without committing to an agreement, your words are only promises that can be broken at any time.

Relationship – People define a relationship in many ways, sometimes even confusing a relationship with friendship.

A relationship is a connection. When two people are involved with each other sexually; you have created an intimate relationship.

(As a teenager, my mother said to me: "If you sleep with him, then you go with him.") I believed my mom then, but Lord knows it's not true today. My, my, my… how time changes our lives.

A safe environment – A man wants to know that his home and family are safe and sound. He wants to come home knowing that he isn't going to be threatened. Anyone can get a house, but the matter is whether that house is a home.

Understanding – Have the intelligence to comprehend. Interpreting and analyzing is part of understanding. You must listen and comprehend in order to provide advice, guidance, and support. Even if you understand but don't agree; (hint) always know you can agree to disagree. A man is more conventional; when he is met at least halfway; instead of just being wrong.

Attention – Hey, everyone wants some attention even men; believe it or not. Compliment your man when it is due. Show some concern, and some interest. Check him out while he is working, sleeping, eating and making love. If love isn't in the air, then just show him that you care. Actions go a long way, ladies.

Listener – Have an ear even when you are not feeling it. A good listener rarely has to second guess, assume or makeup something. When a man speaks, ladies listen…he may very well be trying to tell you something. Not listening makes him think "There is no need to say anything because she isn't listening to me anyways." So, ladies, stop, be patient, and LISTEN.

Independent Woman – An independent woman is confident and can hold a conversation. Men, be careful what you ask for. The need for a woman to be independent can make or break you. An independent woman can handle her own, she is secure, she takes control, and she is positive, confident, and aggressive. These women don't have many needs. However, they are often considered "High Maintenance" and intimidate men easily.

Most men like an independent woman because she has her lifestyle and activities; which give both their space. Men like women who can hold their own; therefore, they are not dependents. The relationship works because they both can come together and spend quality time together.

Note: they both have something going for themselves independently.

Quality Time/Self Time – Everyone, whether in a relationship or not, needs the quality time or time for oneself. Time for no one but you and your partner. Quality time is when you give each other undivided attention and share words, feelings, thoughts, emotions, and intimacy.

It is Appreciated – Being grateful for just having someone special in your life. Appreciate things, gifts, time, or just having a man. There are so many women who want to be appreciated and want to provide appreciation to a man. It's the little things that count, ladies. Today, we are so caught up with high-quality that we don't acknowledge or even care about the little things like a 20 dollar bill. Yeah, yeah... you are probably saying, "What the fuck... Twenty dollars can't buy me anything. He can just as well keep that."

Well, I'm here to tell you, ladies, that a 20 dollar bill can...

Give you a half tank of gas to meet the girls out
for a happy hour.
Pay for your lunch for 2+ days.
Buy you several drinks for happy hour.
Get you a gift card to your favorite store.

Pay for a movie night.

I could go on and on, but you get my point. Even better, give it back to him, when he takes you out for dinner. Use the 20 dollars and pay for the tip. That's showing appreciation. He will be more willing to treat you more often.

Leadership – Well, men, this is a tough one. Being a leader is huge, some big shoes to wear. Many men have failed at this role, and therefore, the women have stepped up to the plate and have taken over. A man trying to get this role back is more challenging, but this is where trust comes in play.

Ladies, give them what they want. If the man fails, then it's up to you to provide them with however many chances you want. (For me, I don't reach strike 3, if you get my drift). You must trust him and let it go. Let the man provide security for the household. TRUST, TRUST, TRUST.

1 Corinthians 11:3: But I want you to understand that the head of every man is Christ, the head of a wife is her husband, and the head of Christ is God.

Support – Ladies, if a man wants to support or be supportive, let him. BEWARE: do this only as long as he isn't giving to receive before you are ready; or giving to control the relationship.

NOTE: Being supportive comes from the heart without a purpose behind it.

Honesty and Health – Honesty is a biggie. When you talk about honesty, it doesn't mean your past. What's in your past, if you are smart, stays in your past. It's what you are looking for in a relationship, setting boundaries, your health, changes, and so on.

Ladies, talk about your health problems. Men need to know that *menopause* exists in life and how it changes your life. Men know what they are used to receiving. They don't think about time, getting older or the body changing. Let it be known, once you hit the 40 to 50 age range, that it's time to have an honest, educational conversation about the big "M."

Men need to know you might feel tired, sad, or undesirable; you might have mood swings you might seem to be unable to get motivated, you might experience dryness and a decrease in your sex drive. But don't feel bad about it because men are menopausal as well. Most men have the same symptoms as women but not as sudden. Their decrease in testosterone causes tiredness, sadness, lack of energy, a reduction in their sex drive, and erectile dysfunction.

Don't point the finger, because it goes both ways. Discuss how to handle and deal with the situation. This could make your relationship much stronger.

When I was much younger, I heard a funny statement that men would say. "I'll trade you in for a newer model car." I used to laugh because that was the same as, "I am going to get rid of your old tail for a younger woman." Well, here is the thing, what makes a man think a newer model wants an old driver? Because if Mama is old; then he is too.

CHAPTER 5

My Opinion on the 90-Day Rule

First, I would like to give honor and respect to Steve Harvey for the person he is and his life accomplishments.

I respect Steve's views and reasons for the 90-day rule. I personally feel that the 90-day rule applies more to single women in the dating field looking for a committed relationship.

I feel at a certain point and time in a woman's life, putting time on her cookie is for the birds. When two adults are together, and the emotions, passions and physical attractions are there, the curiosity of wanting to be intimate, breaks the 90-day rule.

What is the difference in the 90-day rule of getting "A Good Man" versus holding your cookie as a punishment or a payback to discipline the man? Understanding the strategy behind the 90-day rule makes a difference in knowing when to utilize the rule; otherwise, the rule becomes a game for the man to see how long it takes to get the cookie.

The 90-day method is for those who have tried everything to get and keep a man and still ended up single and alone. For those of you who fall into this category, the method is to take the time to help you to analyze yourself and determine your change in motivating and building your self-esteem to heal the bad experience(s) you have encountered in life. If sex is an activity you have been giving to men while dating, make a change and hold back on that at the beginning of your dating or relationship.

Now, don't get it twisted; it's not a tool to use against the man. Don't think if he waited for 90-days one time; you can use it on him other times, such as when the two of you have an argument or disagreement, and you think you can get mad and decide to hold off the cookie for 90-days as payback or punishment. Ladies, the payback or punishment may very well backfire on you and bring hurt to you for 190 days or more. You have only created the beginning of a broken relationship or marriage. Think about it…

Ladies, the 90-day rule does not stop you from getting your feelings hurt. It only helps a man draw conclusions about you. You really do not want a man to see you as controlling and selfish or to think that he is being punished for what some other man did to you. If rules are on the line, let them be agreed on between the two of you and not between you and a book.

If you just want to wait to get to know the man better, then that is a good reason but doing it just because a book says to do it is not good. If there is a physical attraction, I say follow your heart. You can't go wrong, because you did what you wanted to do, whether you waited one day, one week, one month or one year. DO YOU!!!

Waiting 90-days also may depend on the man. He might wait and he might not. If he faithfully waits, you better thank God.

I personally don't think a man is going to wait for 90-days. I honestly would not want to be put on probation for 90-days as an adult while dating. If he has in mind to put me on a 90-days waiting period, he surely better not tell me, because I'm kissing home boy good-bye.

If the man is willing, well let's say…he'll tell you that he is ready to wait 90-days. All along he is getting a cookie on the outside. After 90-days, he'll be all over you because curiosity will be about to kill him. You decide it's time because 90 days have passed. You give him the cookie, and it isn't what he expected…guess what??? He is going right back to the cookie he was hitting while you had him waiting.

Better yet ladies, on the other hand, what if you waited for 90-days and you had sex, after that, and it wasn't right for you. He couldn't get or keep an erection; he was small and short, he was lazy, his movement sucked, and so on. Remember, you were the one who imposed the 90-day rule on him. Now, the man is feeling you emotionally and physically. He thought the sex was just great and is feeling you even more than ever. He is happy and ready to go to the next level because he feels he has a full package. Now, what are you going to do??? Let me guess…

Call your girlfriend and tell her how bad the sex was.

Act as if you are still interested in him but want him to go away.

Let him continue to give you gifts, and wine and dine you.

Jump back into the free and single lifestyle.

Start hanging with the girls again at the same time looking for someone else, hoping he gets the picture because you are not spending time with him.

Start lying and cheating, ducking and dodging because you don't want to hurt his feelings.

Today, many relationships are broken because people stay together for the wrong reasons such as sex, money, and control. These are significant reasons for cheating and how cheating gets started.

My point is there is nothing wrong with having protected sex with a man while dating or in a relationship because (1) you two are still learning about each other (2) if the sex doesn't meet your standards, it's still early enough in the relationship to talk about it and determine if it's workable or if you both should move on; and (3) you both still have respect, pride, and dignity.

The bottom line is to go with your feelings and follow your heart. If your feelings and heart take you to the bedroom, just prepare yourself for the consequences. We are very connected to our emotions, and once we are intimate, we immediately want to attach ourselves to the man. STOP!!! Slow down and enjoy the dating/relationship time

CHAPTER 6

The 80/20 Rule in a Relationship

The 80/20 Rule was established as the Pareto principle, or "the Power Law." It says that 80 percent of the effects come from 20 percent of the causes. This equation doesn't mean 80 percent and 20 percent equal 100 percent. It means that it is not uniform, meaning your relationship is unbalanced, unequal, and problematic.

In a relationship, the 80/20 rule symbolizes that you get only 80 percent of what you need or want, and the other 20 percent comes from someone else providing what you are looking for or missing in a relationship, meaning 9 out of 10 times the 20 percent will allow your partner to cheat or become infatuated with other avenues and maybe lead to divorce or separation.

The Pros and Cons of the 80/20 Rule in a Relationship

The 80/20 rule has its benefits in a relationship. The 80 percent is the best part because it's the excitement of having a new partner that has new ideas, passions, interests, and sexual enjoyment, just loving every moment with each other. Truthfully, we all practice the 80/20 rule in relationships and may not even know. We start by getting to know our mate. You contribute a lot of your time, respect, energy, money, trust, feeling, honesty, and past experiences. As the relationship develops, you think you know everything about your mate; to realize that issues have started to occur, and you now see how your mate deals with disagreements. The 20 percent is dealing with the unknown or unexpected. Most will go on to fulfill that issue with satisfaction and pleasure because they are quick to think, "I'm not dealing with that shit. We are not compatible." You start looking, socializing, and you get caught up because your mate is still waiting to deal with the problems that transpired.

    The correct action to take is to handle your business and deal with the problems because you still have growth in your relationship. Communication is the solution to any problem. You can compromise and agree to disagree. Running and searching for a spare is not a solution; it's a problem. You are only creating problems by sneaking out to see the one providing the 20 percent you think you are missing. That 20 percent is called cheating and is confusing. You confuse yourself because now what are you going to do? Do you let the 80 percent go for 20 percent? You better think hard about that question.

    I think it's always hard to start over with a new mate. You might think you know that person with 20 percent, but you also have to learn the other 80 percent of that person.

An excellent solution to the 80/20 rule is to be realistic about knowing that no one gets exactly what they want. When you are getting to know your partner, ensure you learn about him or her to the fullest; that way you will know exactly what you are getting. You then realize you can't get what he or she doesn't have; find a solution between the two of you and be happy. What's the old saying? "If it's not broke don't fix it," meaning if your relationship is working, there is no need to change it. In finding a resolution, don't blame your partner, continue the relationship growth, and just go with it.

Ladies and gentlemen, make sure you are giving whatever percentage you are requesting. Focus on the positive in your relationship; instead of focusing on the negative. Life is too short to waste. Count your blessings and be happy.

I have to add this: we are so hung up on physical attraction, that love can be looking you right in your face, but you can be blind to it because of beauty and reasons like these:

He has to be built and muscular.

He needs to wear a suit and dress shoes with an office job.

He has to be tall, dark and handsome.

He has to go to the gym.

He can't look too old.

He can't have a stomach

She must be small built.

She must have long hair.

She has to be outgoing.

She must be independent.

She must be neat and clean.

She can't be fuller than I want my woman

These are just a few of the things I have come across, especially on dating sites. Well, that is why those people are still out there looking for love. They are looking for the wrong attractions. By nature, we have a tendency to judge by physical attraction, by what we see, more than by what we know about a person. I know looks play a significant role in the selection, but it's the heart that will make you happy not the looks. Good looks can and will make you miserable because you will be too busy looking to see who else is looking at what you have, to the point that you will be unhappy and making your partner miserable.

If you are looking for physical attraction in a person, you are not looking for love. You are lusting. Lusting is an emotion or feeling of intense desire in the body. Lust is selfish, possessive, and greedy.

Don't let trivial attractions be the missing 20 percent in your relationship. Truthfully, those hang-ups are not worth a conversation; nor a reason to cheat or leave.

CHAPTER 7

For the Love of Money and for the Love of Fame

For the love of money is known to be the root of evil. First, I have to say; if you can't talk to your partner about money and debt, your relationship is already over. It is known that money is the leading cause of arguments, breakups, and divorces in relationships.

There are three main essential factors in a relationship, and they are: communication, money, and sex. I think while dating it's always a plus to talk money…do the what-if scenarios. For example, ask your mate "If we lived together, how would you handle the financial budget?" This will determine if he or she is right for you. If the answer is, "You would have your account, and I would have mine." Let that selfish soul go!

Money is sensitive to most people because we all work hard for our money and want to ensure it is managed correctly. Well, we all know women think about things most men do not. We like to look good, live well and still have money in the bank. Most men want to look good, have a nice ride and spend money.

Saving can be more difficult for them. Do you see the night and day there?

I recommend that when you are in a relationship, you determine which of you is most reliable in the financial area. That person should have more responsibility for maintaining the bills. There should be four accounts: (1) the account where all money is deposited, (2) the emergency account (3) his account and (4) her account or use a similar budget program that will work for you both. Remember that once you marry, you become one.

Once the bills are paid out of the first account, a set percentage should go toward the emergency account and the remaining distributed between his and her account. Now, it will not always be a 50/50 split between his and her account, because one may request more for expenses such as transportation. Do you get my point? This is mainly for those who are married or living together and working toward marriage.

Hey, I didn't forget: if you blow your money; it wouldn't be fair to dig into the emergency account or take your partner's money without an agreement between the two of you. If you take without permission, then guess what: you are stealing. You have broken the trust in the relationship; which is another problem.

"For the love of money" is a dangerous game people play. The Bible states:

1 Timothy 6:9-10 But they that will be rich fall into temptation

and a snare, and into many foolish and hurtful lusts, which drown men in destruction and perdition.

For the love of money is the root of all evil: which while some coveted after, they have erred from the faith, and pierced themselves through with many sorrows.

Hebrews 13:5 Let your conversation be without covetousness; and be content with such things as ye have: for he hath said, I will never leave thee, nor forsake thee.

Money can buy you goods, and services and pay debts, but for sure you can't buy love or happiness.

Celebrities often get caught up in the love of money and fame. The power of money drives them and their lives until reality catches up with them. Many adults can't handle the stress and the price they have to pay to keep the image of being rich and famous.

Also, youths who have a career in the popular lifestyle are good at their role; but are unaware of the future consequences of having money and fame. Once they become considered adults, they struggle to live normal lives. This is because they never had the opportunity to live a normal childhood, which many never get over. As parents who live the fame lifestyle seem to be more focused on keeping up with the "Jones" rather than living a healthy real life.

The tragedy resulting from the love for money, riches, and fame could result in death. Many of our loved ones didn't survive this lifestyle but tried everything they could to cope with the stress.

CHAPTER 8

The Dos in a Relationship…

Put forth an effort. Anything worth having is worth fighting for. Put some energy into your relationship; that way you can get some energy out of it.

Communicate and listen. This is a two-way street. If you want someone to communicate with and listen to you; then you have to return the favor.

Take it slow. There is no need to rush anything worth having. Take it slow and grow together.

Always provide him with compliments. Hey, we all like compliments, especially when they make us feel good and build self-esteem.

Be spontaneous and surprise him with gifts. It doesn't have to be a new suit or a new pair of shoes. A lovely gift could be as simple as a CD of his favorite artist or a charming necktie.

Be honest and truthful. Don't be afraid to talk about the good, bad, right or wrong. No one is perfect; we all make mistakes; some are bigger than others, but they're still mistakes.

Be patient. If it's going to be, it will be. Don't force anything, because you will push your partner right out of your life. Forcing your partner is a red flag because he then starts to wonder why. He may think *hmm...she must be in debt, or maybe there is another side to her, and she can't pretend any longer.* So be careful what you ask for.

Be forgiving and responsible. Never be too big or proud to forgive. When you don't forgive, you carry that guilt around and never have closure. As adults, everyone is responsible for his or her own action(s). The #1 action in a relationship or marriage is to be or become friends.

Find interest in one or more of his hobbies. Be involved but be limited in your involvement. Be willing to participate in something he enjoys.

Always have trust until it's broken. If he breaks the trust and he is worth keeping; find it in your heart to forgive and move forward.

Let him know how you are feeling. Everyone has something to bring to a relationship. His something may not be a healthy bank account. Don't be greedy or blind; there are many qualities he could have, such as:

Having a loving heart or, being a great cook, a family man, a maintenance man, a great lover, or intelligent. He could have cleaning skills, or he could be passionate and inspirational. He could even have a little bit of money but remember, money can't buy you love. So, focus on other values and capabilities.

Show some independence. Men love when a woman is independent; it takes a lot of stress off of them. Always take time for yourself; if nothing else take time to check you where you are, where you want to be, and how can you get there.

Make the necessary changes in your life that work for both of you. Have no fear just enjoy your life. Don't let your significant changes be for the worst. Change is a positive act in a relationship. Change is to make the two of you happy with a secure foundation.

Keep your relationship issues to yourself. The more of your business you tell, the worse your relationship gets. When you tell others your business, you are involving them in your relationship. Everyone needs someone to talk to and open up to but limit your circle. Choose one good friend, no more than two.

People have a tendency to judge and use your information against you. BE CAREFUL IN WHO YOU CHOOSE TO BE YOUR FRIEND.

Whatever you do, please don't put your relationship difficulties in the media. This is a wrong move because some family members and friends are just waiting to gossip. If you need to talk, talk to your partner.

Leave your past in the past. Whatever happened between you and your ex, find closure. Pain is like a sore, a scab that forms and falls off when a new layer of skin forms. You forget all about the pain of the sore and go on about your business, but you try your hardest not to do what you did to cause another sore. Well, as I see it…old relationships are the same. You get hurt, it heals, you move on, but you learned a lesson from it.

The lesson is not to repeat it. Take time to examine what happened and why it happened so that you don't repeat it in your new relationship or marriage.

Don't get angry and hold onto it; because that's unhealthy. Don't take it out on the next man that comes your way. listen, ladies here is the deal… if the man is gone, let him go and be glad he is gone because he wasn't the one God has planned for you. You went through the hurdles because he is preparing you for the man he has chosen for you.

Be HAPPY. Pharrell said it best: "Be happy if you feel like happiness is the truth; be happy if you know what happiness is to you. Be happy if you feel like that's what you wanna do."

We have so much in life to be happy about. Life is too short to worry about what you no longer have. Be happy about what you are about to get. There are some good men out there waiting to find their queen. Be happy and be ready.

Be satisfied. So many women have a man, some have a good man yet are not happy. The more the man does, the more the woman wants. Be satisfied that you have a man in your life. So many of us are looking for a good man. There is a massive shortage of men, so take it from me and be satisfied with what you have. Enjoy the passion, fun, intimacy and quality time. TRUST ME.

Be open-minded. Be ready and willing to entertain new ideas, views, discussions, bedroom positions, and so on. Be positive and say yes, let's do it. Flexible is good but be honest as well. If you are not comfortable with something, speak up and tell him. You never know… he might feel the same and wanted to feel you out.

Establish limitations and boundaries. This is when you say NO. All relationships should have limitations. Enough is enough; NO means NO, don't cross the line, and so on. Set your boundaries in the beginning; there is nothing wrong with that. You are basically letting him know what you are willing to do and what you are not willing to do. He can only accept, respect and honor your boundaries. Now he knows where you stand, and if your limitations or boundaries are violated, then he has created a problem in the relationship.

Be understanding. Listen, comprehend and provide positive feedback.

Be loyal. Be devoted and faithful in your relationship to the best of your ability. Hey, if you are feeling lonely, neglected, or unfulfilled, speak up and let him know what you are feeling. If you let it go…you may be letting him go because you are lonely. Nine out of 10 times, he is too. Two lonely people end up with one being happy meaning someone else is making him happy. Check yourself.

Be caring. Be supportive. Show that you care about him, his decisions, his friendship and that you care for him just the way he is.

Show much love; cuddle, hug, kiss, and hold hands. Actions speak louder than words. Happiness is a beautiful feeling. Make it your routine to show some love. God gave us a gift to love one another, so put it to use, especially when you are receiving love back.

Have faith and belief. Give him a chance. Have faith in his decisions and values. Believe in him with confidence. If it's not there, it will show.

Dream and be ambitious. Look at where you are in your relationship, decide where you want to be and strive for it. Talk to him. See if he is on the same page and goes from there. Have a goal the two of you can work on together. Dream together and be connected.

CHAPTER 9

The Don'ts in a Relationship...

Never leave your partner without a hug and kiss.

Don't expect a perfect relationship. If you find an ideal man, run because no one is perfect. Having little disagreements in a relationship is healthy. You can agree to disagree, and both will be content. This is another way to get to know your partner.

Don't be a nagger. Nagging ruins everything in a relationship. First of all, he is not your child. Second, he will shut down and tune you out; which means you are wasting your time nagging. Third, he will find a peaceful place to go, and that could be the end of your relationship.

Don't accuse unless you have facts. Typically, when you start accusing, it's because you may be the one who is doing the cheating. The insecurity of not being caught makes people think that they can cheat and not get caught as well.

Don't be controlling. This is a sign of guilt, making something out of nothing. If you know that this is you, get some help before you try to have a relationship.

Don't forget to say something sweet every day.

Don't stop dating your man. When you have a good day, surprise him, and ensure he is having a good day and a good night too.

Don't use the 90-day rule. Start it right with a compromised decision. A relationship is about two people, not one person.

Don't be jealous and overly protective. This is a sign of insecurity. Don't bring your past into the relationship. Everyone deserves a chance to prove you wrong. Think positive.

Don't be selfish. It's the two of you and not all about you. A one-sided relationship has never begun. You are a problem all by yourself; therefore, you really do not want anyone else.

Don't cheat; be open and honest.

Don't claim everything by saying, "Mine." If you are in a relationship, it's no longer yours; therefore, be partners and say, "Ours."

Don't call him other than his birth name or belittle him. This makes him fragile, lowers his confidence and ruins the relationship.

Don't let your baby momma/daddy drama take over your relationship. Communicate! Have respect; remember the kids are the innocent ones, and most of all they come first.

Don't lie, just tell the truth and deal with the consequences later. We never want to hear negative or shocking words, but just know that the truth is coming out and it's not the end of the world.

Don't be afraid to share your feelings because you are afraid of getting hurt. God puts no more on us than we can bear.

Don't treat him differently around your friends or family than you do when the two of you are alone.

Don't use your "cookie" as a punishment. This right here will get you nowhere in a relationship. What it does is open the door for someone else to enter into the relationship. (What's the saying? What you won't do, someone else will).

Don't break a commitment that you have made. Once you break a promise, you have planted a seed of distrust. Once a person loses trust in you, it's very hard to get it back.

Don't take advantage of his kindness or weakness. Hey, God doesn't like ugly. Taking advantage of someone is a selfish and unacceptable act. Instead, why not be kind and appreciative of them?

Don't complain about problems; find solutions. Whatever you are complaining about, 9 times out of 10, you can solve the problem yourself. Just suck up your pride and do it yourself. It won't hurt, just thank God you can do something yourself.

Don't fall in love overnight; take your time. Don't be so quick to show him what you are capable of doing in bed. Let his imagination take him for a ride. This will only make him wonder about you and appreciate you more. Always hold onto something of intimate value. Don't show it all at once. If he is not the right one, then my saying is he didn't get all of you.

Don't compare your ex to the man you are in a relationship with. Comparing the past man to the future man is an enormous sign that you are not over your ex, especially if you are doing this regularly. You must find closure from your past to have a future relationship.

Don't play childish games. He's a man, not a child. Anyone can get tired of playing a game; at some point, the game ends. Hint, hint!

Don't ever fall asleep mad because tomorrow isn't promising. The bible says:

Ephesians 4:26-27: Be angry and do not sin; do not let the sun go down on your anger, and give no opportunity to the devil.

Don't let problems get old. Deal with them as they occur. You don't go back and dig up old issues. What's in the past stays in the past.

Don't be afraid of change. Change is suitable for everyone. If everything stays the same, then your relationship will get old, tired and in trouble.

Don't involve yourself in his business unless he asks you. Be respectful; but also, be supportive.

Don't bring your friends and family members in your relationship. You have to be able to separate the two. If you are in a relationship; your friends and family should respect that and give you space. Friends and family can sometimes be your worst enemy. Misery likes company. Your girlfriend is someone you confide in and who knows your man because you tell her your business. She could very well be waiting for you to end the relationship so she can move in and take your man because she knows what you didn't do and what your man needs and wants.

Don't feel the need to be with him 24/7. Smothering is aggravating. Choose a hobby and give the man some space. It's healthy for both of you.

Don't assume anything. Assumptions don't get you anywhere even if they're true. You must be sure that they are.

Don't let your emotions dictate or control your relationship, conversations or arguments. Ladies, we are emotional by nature and have less control over our feelings than men; therefore, we should identify our emotions, accept them and talk them out with our partner.

Don't put pressure on the man. Pressuring a man is a negative action, and he will only get tired of the stress and flee.

I've listed some valuable shortcomings. Ask yourself… would you be happy if a man exercised any of these shortcomings in your relationship? I know your answer is no. Now, if you find yourself performing any of my don'ts, please stop now and check yourself. Get some counseling as soon as possible (ASAP).

CHAPTER 10
What Does it Take to Save Your Relationship?

The first step of saving a relationship is the two parties wanting to keep the relationship. You have to decide whether your relationship is worth saving. If you are the one fighting in your relationship and your partner is not fighting for the relationship as well, the answer is straightforward, just let it go and move on. If the two of you want to save your relationship and are willing to fight to keep it; then it is time to analyze your connection. I believe in the pen and paper method; write it down. Get a sheet of paper and write on one side the good in the relationship and on the other side write the bad in the relationship. If the good outweighs the bad, he is a keeper. If the bad outweighs the good, then let him go.

In the movie, *Why Did I Get Married,* Janet Jackson's character had her friends write a list of the good and the bad things they saw in their husbands. I thought that was the best solution to save their marriages, and it worked.

Ladies and gentlemen, we all know that a relationship is

a part-time job. It's something you are continually working toward. Continuously trying to find motivational activities; volunteering outings and gatherings; learning about yourself and your partner; having role responsibilities; having individual duties; interviewing and learning by communicating; making time for each other and being cautious of the competitors. It's a challenge all by itself.

If you have it in your heart to make it work, the effort is worth the challenge. Keep it clean, dedicated, and honest, and you will be happy, but always remember the old saying: "What goes around; comes around." This can play a part in your relationship hurdles. If you cheated in the past and now you are ready to commit, just know that the relationship may not be perfect because what goes around, comes around. I want to express that no one is perfect, and shit happens. Don't let one mistake ruin a great relationship. Handle your business and roll with it; forgive and forget. Remember what I said, "It's not the end of the world." Look at it as payback and be forgiving. On the other hand, if the cheating happens multiple times, move on because there is someone else who deserves you. Move on.

As bad as it may sound, it's not hard to forgive. God is a forgiving God because we all make mistakes. Once you forgive, that is just the beginning. You have many more steps to take, because if you forgive, you leave it, chop it up and throw it away. If you do not, you are setting yourself up for reoccurrence and pain.

Once you forgive, you must have a conversation about how it happened, when it happened, where it happened and why it happened. You need to know what went wrong and how to fix it.

You must start by coming clean and telling the truth. The truth will hurt, but it will set you free. Accept the fact that you messed up and are willing to make it right but never go down that road again. You must do whatever it takes to keep the love of your life, if your partner is the love of your life.

If you cheated with a co-worker, be willing to look for another job. Cut the ties or decide to relocate. You must communicate and open up because if your partner had something to do with your cheating, he or she deserves to know what he or she needs to do to improve and to prevent this from happening again.

Most individuals don't want to tell the truth because they do care and don't want to hurt their partner's feelings, but I'm here to tell you, that it's better to tell him or her the truth before someone else does. No matter what, it's going to hurt, but trust me it hurts worse when it comes from an outsider who knows your business. At that point it doesn't just hurt, it's embarrassing and humiliating.

Sit down and talk about it because communication time is needed. The hurt, pain, and embarrassment won't go away overnight. Patience steps in. Find it in your heart if you want to save your relationship. Take it slow and start over. Start slow.

Ladies, we have a tendency to slack when it comes to keeping our man happy. We get relaxed after being with a man for some time. When your situation is at this point, there's nothing wrong with dating your man all over again.

Stop the nagging and step up to the plate. Show him that you still have it and can love again. Bring your sexy back to the bedroom. Choose a night for fun and start that day first thing in the morning. Make a couple of calls during the day letting him know that you can't wait to see him and how much you miss him. Get a love card and have it on the bed when he gets home. Get a sexy lingerie outfit and have it on when he gets home with matching high heels. Have some candles, wine, and your toys ready to go. Forget everything and everybody and make your night work for you and him.

When I say this, I'm not talking about being "selfish." I'm talking about enjoying and pleasing yourself too while enjoying and pleasing your partner.

Look here…ladies and gentlemen. There is no need for making love or having sex if you are not feeling it. Why? Because no matter what, you won't be happy or satisfied. This is a mistake many couples make in a relationship because they think the other party wants to interact; so, they do it for their partner. That's a "no, no." If you can't give your all, then don't give any. Why waste your time and energy getting dirty and feeling upset?

Trying to save your relationship takes the effort of both parties.

Quality time is time; no one can take from you. It should involve some exceptional moments. If you are requesting quality time, then you are the one who is supposed to make that time valuable. Set the level and standards for that time. I call my quality time a time to treat and be treated. When the evening or night is over, both parties should have big smiles and think they can't wait to do it all over again. The second time should be even better. Never have a repeated night no matter how good it was. Why? Because repeats become annoying and nothing is exciting to look forward to. Always add a little spice and fun in your bedroom.

Just a little encouragement, baby oil works wonders. Give each other a total body massage, to start the night in a significant way. I'm just saying… two can have a great romantic night, but you don't have to engage in sex. Hey, if it happens, roll with it, if not you can still say, it was enjoyable.

Another activity is taking weekend trips. Get out of the house. Driving will allow for some communication time. The conversation doesn't have to always be about a problem. Talking about solutions is nice. The one thing I will say is never let your relationship get old and settled. Come up with new ideas and activities. Get your partner engaged, let him, or her make decisions on what action to do next. Laugh and talk about old times while relaxing, such as the wedding day/night, the bachelor's party, the first date, and so on. Here's another one, ask each other what your most desirable moments are and make them come true (if this is something you are willing and able to do).

Take the initiative to take the focus off of the relationship for a minute and do something good for yourself. Stand in front of the mirror and ask yourself what you could do to make a change and make yourself feel better. Whatever you do, don't fall into the pity, because no one wants to join a pity party. When one starts to talk about depression, you will be the life of that party, and you will be the conversation after the party. Change is a good thing. It's for your happiness. Never let anyone steal your joy. Like the old saying goes, "Never let them see you sweat." Invest in yourself, just as you should invest in your partner.

Remember with all that's being said; the romance won't save your relationship. Don't just drop and forget what has happened in your relationship. Remember you are trying to keep it. Don't let the romance override the problem. You both still have to communicate and resolve the issues while dating and enjoying one another all over again. It took the two of you to get in the relationship; it will take the two of you to resolve your problems or terminate the relationship.

Find a counselor for relationships or marriage to help determine your differences and find solutions to save your relationship. In the meantime, show each other love and respect. Also, try to find quality time to discuss what went wrong. The discussion will give your counselor something to start with.

Start by discussing the reasons you married your partner in the beginning, whether it was for love, companionship, children, or another reason.

I think the best counseling is held between you and your partner. The problems started with the two of you. Each of you knows what you did or did not do. Each knows the other's personality, weaknesses, and strengths. Try to solve your problems before spending money on a counselor.

CHAPTER 11

How to Determine When it's Time to Depart?

Many people are in relationships and marriages but are not happy. When you have given your all, and counseling hasn't resolved your problems, ask God to reveal to you what else you can do to save your relationship, and God shows an open door. This is when it's time to depart. Walk through the door and don't look back.

God said "Let not your hearts be troubled. Believe in God; believe also in me." (John 14:1)

No one should remain in an unhealthy, unsafe, and unhappy relationship. Some people don't know when or how to leave a relationship. There are many indications that you should leave.

You're experiencing physical abuse. "Physical abuse" is when your partner puts his or her hands on you and causes you pain. Know that if it happens once and you accept it, it will definitely happen again. Never let it get to this point, "You can do bad all by yourself." There are plenty of good men and women available. When you think you have the perfect partner; you wake up in a violent situation. Just know that love isn't painful. If your partner loves you, they won't abuse you. (Remember that.)

Drugs have become a problem. "Drug addiction" is when using becomes a habit or pattern. Addicts' behavior changes for the worse. Your partner may become unpredictable and uncontrollable. Many things can happen at this point such as bills not getting paid, miscommunication, attitude, stress, violence, cheating, reduced sexual activity, and so on.

Many people drink alcohol when problems occur in their relationship. Alcohol is like a drug; it changes the emotional state of mind, making you braver rather than sober.

You're experiencing "mental abuse." You don't know if you are going or coming. You are blamed for things that you know you didn't do or say, but you question yourself… wondering if you really did do or say them You are unhappy and can't be the happy person you usually are. You don't want to be around friends or go to work. You want to figure out what is going on. Now you are depressed.

You get depressed it's time to regroup, step back, and clear your head. Once depression kicks in, the problems get worse because now it's affecting your health. You don't have the strength or desire to do anything. You feel alone because your partner is not a partner. You don't have an appetite; you can't sleep; you feel miserable. Stop here and decide whether the relationship is worth it and how you are feeling about it. You must make positive changes in your life starting with what makes you happy.

The wedding ring is gone. If the ring comes off, what are you waiting for? It's time to move on because it's obvious your partner did. No ring means available: get it?

Your partner asks for a separation or divorce. A separation is a time needed to collect thoughts and feelings. Even dating again could play a role in the separation stage if both partners are willing. Divorce means your partner wants to terminate the marriage, to no longer have an agreement, to move on; he or she is letting it go; leaving; saying good-bye for good; meaning that the love is gone, all of the above. I learned from Judge Toler that you never let your partner tell you he or she doesn't want or love you twice. Once is enough, move on. There is a better side of life.

You feel you have nothing else to live for. This is the breaking point. Never feel you have nothing else to live for. God gave you life, and until your time comes, you have so much to live for. You have not accomplished the mission God put you here to do. At this point, your first step to recovery and reality is to get some help and move onto life's enjoyments.

Your partner becomes your roommate. Your partner is no

longer your partner when sex rarely happens, and there is no interaction when it does. You no longer communicate with each other. His or her friends are a priority instead of you. The kids are the friends instead of you. Oh yeah, you have separate banking accounts. You divide the household bills. You have separate bedrooms, and there is little to no concern about what, when, where and how. The question is, are you really happy?

You don't have a voice in the house. You can't speak, think or be heard in your home, around friends or anywhere. Your partner talks for you and makes decisions for you; tells you what to do, and so on. The right partner will allow you to have an opinion and value it.

Money replaces your life. This can lead to abuse in a relationship because when the money isn't there, the anger stimulates an argument and fights begin. Let it be known:

Hebrews 13:5: Keep your life free from the love of money, and be content with what you have.

Ecclesiastes 5:10: Whoever loves money never has money enough; whoever loves wealth is never satisfied with his income. This too is meaningless.

You want to leave, but you stay for material things or your children. If you are in a bad marriage or relationship meaning arguing, fighting, screaming and other abnormal behaviors, this is not healthy, safe or stable for the children.

Children feed off of their parents and acknowledge what they hear and see.

When I was growing up, my parents fussed and fought. My siblings and I felt in control and would ask for things they probably would have said no to, but because of the conflicts, they would always say yes. This was because they could not focus on us and didn't want to deal with additional stress.

Children can be more affected by parents staying together when they should not because they start to act out for attention in school. Their behavior changes; they can become withdrawn from other children.

This is a hard decision to make, but if the parents are not happy, then the children are not happy. This is a good time for parental counseling.

The respect goes down the drain, and there is none left. If there is no respect, there is no love; therefore, there is no marriage or relationship. It's time to go before it gets worse and harm is eventually done.

You are betrayed – If you love your partner, then how many times that you know of did it occur in your marriage or relationship? If this is the first time and you both want to stay together, then forgive them. If it is a reoccurrence, then say goodbye because it won't be the last time.

There is jealousy in the relationship. Jealousy is not a sign of love; don't get it twisted. It's a sign of insecurity and danger.

If your partner is jealous to the point that you are miserable and unhappy, you should let him or her know that if the jealousy continues, you are leaving. If the jealousy continues, then you better go because violence comes next.

If the relationship or marriage counseling is worthless and there are no improvements. Leave.

If rehab doesn't help, leave.

Sometimes departing or separating is a wake-up call and the partner that wants to leave will have time to think about the good, bad and ugly. He or she may seek help and be ready to come back with changes in place.

One thing is for sure; you will know when it's time to let the relationship go. It's when you have reached the last straw.

The last straw is when you cannot and will not put up with your problems any longer.

CHAPTER 12

Did You Give Up Without a Fight?

This chapter is based on interviews with four diversified females and four diversified males who have lived with their partners for more than ten years or who have experienced a divorced marriage. I asked these questions:

How did the relationship begin?

How did time take its toll on the relationship?

How did the relationship end?

Was the breakup mutual or did one of you fight to keep the relationship?

Interviewee #1

Q: How did the relationship begin?

A: I met my ex-husband through my brother. My ex saw me in the elevator and inquired about who I was. After finding out who

I was, he asked my brother to introduce us. From then on we started dating, and the dating became serious. I had a daughter from a previous relationship, and I wanted to know how he would interact with her. That relationship worked out well. After dating for three years, we got married.

Q: How did time take its toll on the relationship?

A: Well, my husband is a good-looking man, and he is very flirtatious. People take his kindness for weakness, and he uses that basically to get what he wants. During the marriage, I would always have to tell him that someone was flirting with him or he was flirting with that person. At first, it used to be a fun game of tit for tat. For example: See who you can get, and I'll see who I can get.

The tit for tat became a severe problem in the marriage when I found out that he cheated behind my back throughout the marriage. After I confronted him and the lady about their affair, he then wanted to work on our relationship. I was also in agreement about working on our relationship. While we were working on our relationship, one of the things he wanted me to do was to come clean; so, he came clean, first revealing outside affairs behind my back. So, I came clean as well, and it turned out we both cheated. From this point in our relation time took its toll once I became pregnant. He then began to act like a fool because he could not accept my flaws. He used my honesty against me. Therefore, he started neglecting me while I was carrying our baby. While I was left at home, he started hanging out nights with friends or his father who also had marriage problems with his wife.

We lived in Germany during our marriage; which was even more difficult for me because that was not home. During his happy hour nights, he met another woman and had an affair, once again. I found out, and he decided to leave the children and me to live in the barracks to continue his relationship with the other woman.

After counseling, the counselor and the military decided to send me home to the States for my best interest. I returned home with my children and without my husband. He stayed in Germany until he was discharged. Once he was released, he returned to the States, apologizing and wanting to work on our relationship. I forgave him, and we reunited while working on our relationship. He stayed home until he found a job while I attended school. We stayed together for approximately three more years.

Q: How did the relationship end?

A: After a total of nine years in the relationship, I forgave and forgot to find out that he once again cheated on me. He once again decided to inform me that he was going to leave. This time I spoke up and said, "If you walk out you can never come back, and this will be the end of our relationship," due to your infidelity.

Q: Was the breakup mutual or did one of you fight to keep the relationship?

A: I was willing to fight for our marriage because of the kids, but I was not willing to deal with the infidelity.

On the other hand, he was not willing to fight for our marriage because he wanted his freedom to continue to cheat. If he could have me and I accepted the infidelity and cheating, then he would have both. Basically, he wanted to have his cake and to eat it too.

Interviewee # 2

Q: How did the relationship begin?

A: I met her at my mother's bar.

Q: How did time take its toll on the relationship?

A: As time went by our relationship was off and on for many years. We both were involved with someone else but not in serious relationships. I must admit that I'm in love with this woman. I wish I had met her first; but neither of us saw the relationship going anywhere, at first.

Q: How did the relationship end?

A: It hasn't ended. We are still very close and the best of friends.

Q: Was the breakup mutual or did one of you fight to keep the relationship?

A: I fought to continue our friendship if not our relationship. I would not stop calling or looking for her. I will never give up on this woman. She is the best woman I've ever come across. One of these days, I will be with her.

Interviewee #3

Q: How did the relationship begin?

A: I was at a night club working the bars, and these handsome men were standing at the door. This particular one was dressed in a suit. He had green eyes and a very nice smile with a gold tooth. In other words, tall and handsome. I asked the owner if he knew him. His response was, "He's a friend of mine." So later that night, he introduced him to me. We talked, and he asked me out on a date.

Q: How did time take its toll on the relationship?

A: As time went on, we continued to date. There were lots of ups and downs. I found out things about this man that took their toll on the relationship. At the same time, he was very good for my child and me by my first marriage. I was hurt by some of the drama that came with him. I questioned our love for each other plenty of times, but I was in a place in my life where he was right for me.

Q: How did the relationship end?

A: This relationship hasn't ended. What happened was he got sick. God and I helped him back where God wanted him to be. He moved in with my daughter and me. We got married. This has been a very good marriage. He is very supportive of anything I do.

Q: Was the breakup mutual or did one of you fight to keep the relationship?

A: There was no breakup, and I didn't have to fight to keep the relationship. This man made sure if I needed anything, he provided it. My place was to be there for him when he needed me. I'm not a fighter; I just treated him good no matter what. Sometimes a man can be turned around only by being with a good woman. We had a child together, which changed him from street affairs.

Interviewee #4

Q: How did the relationship begin?

A: He was friends with my brothers. One day we went walking, and from the walk, a relationship started.

Q: How did time take its toll on the relationship?

A: Over the years the relationship was very stressful. He cheated with multiple women. He didn't want me to go out with friends, but he went out every weekend.

Q: How did the relationship end?

A: I put him out of the house and changed the locks.

Q: Was the breakup mutual or did one of you fight to keep the relationship?

A: The breakup was not mutual, and neither of us fought to keep the relationship.

Interviewee #5

Q: How did the relationship begin?

A: I was going out with his brother in school. I used to babysit for this man and his wife who lived across the street from my parents' house. He and his wife broke up, and she moved out. One day, I was walking home, and he asked me if I wanted a ride home. I said, "Yes unless you have somewhere else to go." He was nine years older than me.

Q: How did time take its toll on the relationship?

A: While in the relationship, he was very jealous. I worked with him hanging sheetrock and spackling apartments as well as houses. When I had to pay the workers, I had to lie and say I put gas in the car so I could go to lunch.

Q: How did the relationship end?

A: It ended when I came back from a trip to New Jersey to see my family and found he cheated on me. He wanted me to stay in New Jersey so he could have his affair. Also, he kept my son. I had to get a lawyer to get my son back along with a divorce. I guess his retaliation was giving me an empty suitcase with no clothes in it.

Q: Was the breakup mutual or did one of you fight to keep the relationship?

A: Yes, I fought to keep the relationship by calling him because I wanted him back even though I would call to make his night unpleasant because of what he had done to me. I also caught him and my sister in bed kissing. So, at that point, my son and I went back to New Jersey to stay. Years later, he came to New Jersey, and we had sexual intercourse together. It was no good, not like it was before; it was totally different. I was glad because experiencing that was how I got over him. He would always say to me that I would be fat and on welfare. I guess I proved him wrong.

Interviewee #6

Q: How did the relationship begin?

A: The relationship began through a friend.

Q: How did time take its toll on the relationship?

A: As time went by, we had many problems. We both were too young with no experience.

Q: How did the relationship end?

A: The relationship ended with her leaving me. Her mother would tell her to leave, and she did.

Q: Was the breakup mutual or did one of you fight to keep the relationship?

A: It wasn't a mutual breakup. I tried to fight to keep her, but it didn't work.

Interviewee #7

Q: How did the relationship begin?

A: We met through his cousin.

Q: How did time take its toll on the relationship?

A: He stressed me out by not working.

Q: How did the relationship end?

A: The relationship ended when I told him to get out.

Q: Was the breakup mutual or did one of you fight to keep the relationship?

A: No, I didn't fight to keep the relationship.

Interviewee #8

Q: How did the relationship begin?

A: It began when I met her at school.

Q: How did time take its toll on the relationship?

A: As the years passed by, I began to have less and less interest in the relationship. We married only because our families forced us to marry.

Q: How did the relationship end?

A: It ended when I took sick with a stroke. She lied about having insurance on me. She left me in the emergency room and said she couldn't take care of me.

Q: Was the breakup mutual or did one of you fight to keep the relationship?

A: No, I didn't fight to keep the relationship, but she tried to get me back after she realized I wasn't dying as the doctors stated. I remarried, and life is excellent.

CHAPTER 13

Why Men Say They Cheat?

I distributed a survey to over 150 men regardless of race, gender, religion, age or disability. In addition to my survey, I interviewed over ten men who are married or have been married at least three times in their life.

Here are the reasons why men say they cheat:

> **SEXUAL BOREDOM** – Men get tired of the same thing over and over, and the thought of a lifetime of boredom probably makes a man seek out a thrill. It may have nothing to do with the woman, i.e., it doesn't mean they no longer like her.
>
> **THRILL OF THE CHASE** – Men like the challenge, the hunt, and the chase. When they've caught their prey, it's over. "Nesting" is not exciting by comparison.
>
> **INABILITY TO COMMUNICATE** – Men who can't express themselves or talk about their needs or feelings may address their dissatisfactions by seeking an exciting

distraction.

LACK OF SELF-AWARENESS – Even more fundamentally, men who have no idea what they are feeling or why, may feel the need to do something, anything, to feel better.

IMMATURITY – The inability to anticipate or care about the consequences of their actions may lead some men to act irrationally or childishly to get what they want.

STUPIDITY – They make bad decisions they possibly regret later.

ASSHOLE-NESS – There is no explanation or rationale. It's just a character flaw.

NO SENSE OF FEAR – Men have no fear of losing the woman they cheat on but fear the woman they don't want to lose.

THE FLESH VERSES THE SPIRITUAL MAN – Some men struggle with their inner being of wanting more and not being satisfied with what God has blessed them with. Men will search for Cinderella in all the wrong places, just looking to fulfill their needs or a way to satisfy their ego. Men just want more; they don't have a purpose or goal for why they want more.

PRO-CREATE – Men are innately born to pro-create, hunt, kill and provide. Being connected to one person gives stability and enhances cultural applications. It does not, however, satisfy the inner cravings.

LACK OF SEX – The woman is bad in bed; there are compatibility issues. She may not be exceedingly sexual or intimate at all; she is prudish or lacks enthusiasm. Lack of enthusiasm translates to lack of skills. Skills in the bedroom are critical to men. In the same vein, a woman can have a normal libido but just not know what she's doing. If he isn't getting it how he likes it, and as often as he likes it, he will cheat.

You start the beginning of the relationship with sexual vibes for months and years then you have given that man a sexual impression. You must continue this, or the man will seek attention somewhere else. Most relationships start well. He or she believes people get complacent as the relationship grows and they forget what brought them together. Among all the excuses that can be made, "*lack of discipline*" is the main reason. Sure, your partner plays a role in your decision-making process, but at the end of the day, the discipline is within yourself. You have a moral decision to make, **"Will I cheat or be faithful?"**

PLENTIFUL – Some men feel that they were put on earth to have as many women as possible.

LACK OF SELF-WORTH – If a man doesn't value himself, he won't value anyone else.

GETTING MARRIED TOO YOUNG AND FOR THE WRONG REASON – One man stated that he cheated on his wife because he wasn't happy and had married for the wrong reason. He married her to prove a point to his mother and father. She is an older woman but a great woman. He loves her but is not in love with her. He said, that after he married, he met another lady whom he had an affair with due to the sensation. He says that after cheating with the same woman for an extended period, it's not the same anymore and then you seek another woman; it's a terrible disease. His sexual relationship with his wife at home isn't the same because he wants more interaction, and that is his main reason for cheating

He concludes, If a man truly loves his woman and she does what she can to keep her man happy, there wouldn't be room or thought outside the box for fornication. It's not always sex, 75 percent of it is when you find the woman that gives you butterflies in your stomach, that makes you weep when you're not near and buy little gifts to make her smile, when she touches you in a way that gives you chills and when she is your best friend.

WOMEN ALLOWING IT – Men cheat because women's standards are so low. Women accept what men put out. Women are their own worst enemy because they are quick to make this statement. "He can do what he wants just as long as he respects me when he is with me."

GREED – Some men like the thrill of having a choice of more than one woman, and not get caught.

AGE – Some men want to see if they still have the play and drive. Most men have a fear of getting old. No matter what it takes, how long it takes, no matter how much money it takes or no matter how hard it is, men will go to the limit to satisfy their egos. Most men do love the woman, but she can't measure up to his ego.

UNFAITHFULNESS OF THE HEART – If men were faithful to themselves, they would in turn release it to their spouse and accept whatever transpires no matter what the cost is. When men cheat, it is a selfish move on their behalf. The heart is deceitfully wicked and is in dire need of cleansing. The flesh has all of those sinful natures built into it, and if your heart is not right, the flesh (dominated by sin) will take charge and cause you to do unrighteous acts. The man has to take charge of his heart and fill it with things that will cause it to make the right decisions.

Is it right to commit adultery? Is it right to fornicate? The flesh says "yes" because the nature of the flesh is never satisfied or content and is magnetized to unrighteousness. If men looked only at the consequences of their unfaithful actions, and not at the in-the-moment experience, it is believed their mindsets would change. Honoring his wife can only happen when a man can place her needs and desires above his own. Remember unselfishness verses unfaithfulness (selfishness).

CONTROL – Men do not have the power they seem to think they have. They rationalize that they love their partners but have anonymous casual sex outside the relationship; which doesn't count. Men cheat because they do not love the one they are with, thinking the grass is greener on the other side.

INTEREST LOSS IN THEIR MATE – Loss of interest can be sex-related, or it can be due to lack of intimacy. Intimacy can be the result of not spending enough time together. How do you keep the interest if you don't spend enough time together? Some men can equate intimacy with gender roles. Is she doing what she is "supposed to?"

Most men want a woman who can cook, clean, takes care of the children, household and the man himself. A man mentality is if you cannot handle and maintain their required duties, then someone else will.

Loss of interest can also be due to appearance. Maybe she doesn't dress how he likes or how she used to dress; perhaps she has gained weight. A man is very visual, and if his wife isn't keeping his interest focused on her, then he will look elsewhere.

DELIBERATELY VIOLATE THE RULES OF A GAME –Men in relationships often use this. "I cheat because that's just part of the game." Think of a good old game of Monopoly, and how you could never go to the bathroom during the game for fear that your opponent might stash a few hundred while you were away. The same rule applies to relationships. To cheat in a relationship is to violate the standards of that relationship. If you have decided as a couple to date exclusively, then any deviation from that rules means you are cheating. According to a recent study on infidelity, roughly 70 percent of men want to cheat, will cheat, or have cheated in their relationship. Now, here is the truth behind the mystery of why.

- He wants to boost his id, not his ego.
- He wants the mere experience of something new/different.
- He wants the thrill of the kill (i.e. Do I still have it?).
- He has insecurity and trust issues.
- He is not being fulfilled sexually by his current partner; the relationship has become banal.
- He believes his significant other will cheat on him or she has cheated in the past.
- He wants to see if he can get away with it.

- He has been offered sex and is too weak to turn it down.
- He believes two is better than one.
- He got away with it before and it was forgiven.
- And finally, he wants to get revenge.

Cheating is much more prevalent than women or men think. For most men, love and sex are two entirely separate things. Men believe this comes from an illogical definition of the word love. His interpretation of cheating is an activity you would not do if your significant other were standing beside you.

VARIETY AND UNFAMILIARITY – It's not about the chase, it's more about the variety or unfamiliarity (big, small, tall, thick, athletic, skinny, etc.). No man wants to get caught up in the drama, and it's certainly not profitable unless she's got some money. A lot of men stop cheating because of the monetary cost involved in cheating that is unless they get caught first. Last but not least, the significant other might not do the same things the side chick does (sexually or mentally).

NOTE: Women are not to be taken lightly. There is a shortage of good men. If a woman has a job with benefits and a car, she is at the top of the backstabber "I want your man list." If your man is one of the weak, help him with the necessary tools from your toolbox. (Give him something to remember when he leaves home). You ladies know, the thing you used to give him, is the same thing you need to use to keep him. Those available women are not joking, they are hungry and have no conscience or respect.

INSECURITY – When a man and a woman start dating, they live separately, they share a lovely relationship and do a lot of things together to get the other person to care. Once they move in together and try to build something more, the relationship changes and her insecurity comes into play, checking calls and contact numbers in the phones, making a point of letting everyone know that he is her man without understanding the relationship of the people who were called. The significant change that comes with living together drives a man away mainly because the woman doesn't have the trust, she claimed to have when they were apart, yet she still wants the man to trust her.

CULTURE – Most men live a lifestyle where what it takes to become a man and gain respect is to be sexually engaging with women. The more women, the more your peers look up to you, and you gain a reputation. The slang term for this is "ladies' man." Once he expands his reputation, a man no longer has to seek a woman; women seek and pursue him. This makes the man feel confident, extraordinary, and free. In doing so, it is beneficial for the man but immoral for the woman. Some women are attracted to such a man, and some are not. Those who are attracted to such behavior are women who do not want to be attached or in a relationship. Once the man is labeled and established as a "ladies' man," whether he gets married or remains single doesn't change his lifestyle, but he shows his wife respect as long as he isn't caught.

The 3Cs will sum it up. (CHASE, CHALLENGE, AND CONQUER).

SELF TENDENCIES – Men want what they want when they want it, and how they want it. Most of the time, they don't even factor in the consequences of their actions. Most times, it just doesn't matter to them. A man's first thought is of a moment of pleasure, instead of the lifelong repercussions.

TOO EASY – Women are easy with the *VAJAYJAY*. If his partner doesn't give a man sex when he wants it, he'll call someone who is more than willing to accommodate his needs.

IN DENIAL – Most men do not consider cheating to be cheating. They think it is how men are made, and as long as the man is taking care of the home, providing for the family, being a good dad, and not running around in the streets with all sorts of women; then he is a good man as if cheating is a reward.

CHAPTER 14

Why Does it Hurt so Bad?

My past long-term relationships hurt when they ended because, at the time, I would think about all the good times we had. The things we did together. The charitable items he provided to me. For me, the worst part was that our time together meant so much to me. I would hurt more when I thought about the time I put into the relationship. Then I thought about why it ended and how I would benefit from it. I always took a positive lesson from the relationships and applied them to the next one. "Lesson learned." But the thought of loneliness would forever crush my heart, I felt empty, knowing I didn't have him in my life anymore. Even though I knew the breakup was for the best, it didn't stop the pain of thinking that I had shared a special part of me and my life with this person.

    I learned that the pain of breaking up comes in stages. (1) pain and emotional confusion. (2) The time needed to get over the relationship. (3) Anger. (4) Analyzing the relationship and problems. (5) Forgiving the other person. And (6) freedom and being ready to move on.

Know that there is no easy way to end a relationship without someone hurting from it. Therefore, whenever there is a good loving relationship, you should prepare yourself mentally in case it goes wrong. This way it will relieve some pain but not all. It will allow you to have a life still and not think it's the end of the world.

Today, it's very, very difficult to find a suitable partner or soul mate, this is another reason it hurts so bad. The thought of having to start all over again is painful and undesirable.

Technology has made breakups even more painful because nowadays, to avoid person to person contact or dealing with seeing the painful hurt of another, one can send a text over the phone. If this should happen to you, please don't be hurt, be happy, because the person who sent the text ending the relationship is less than you are. Therefore, you should thank God it didn't work out and enjoy your life because if the person loved you from the beginning, he or she would at least have given you the respect of having a face-to-face discussion.

Remember, there is someone for everyone, so find your partner and enjoy life.

Pain & Emotional Confusion

The pain and emotional confusion of a broken heart is very unhealthy. The stress causes many health problems, such as heart attacks, depression, anxiety, addiction to alcohol or drugs, and so on.

A breakup is so painful and shocking. One reason is that most times you are blindsided and didn't see it coming. Another reason is that your future, dreams, and plans have all been crushed, you don't know what to do or how to get past it.

We are human beings, and God gave us the heart to love with, but that doesn't mean love will last forever. When putting faith and trust in a relationship, you feel it's forever, and when forever comes sooner than expected, it hurts so bad.

This also causes self-confusion, you start questioning yourself, wondering if you did all the wrong things, wanting a second chance to make it right, blaming yourself, begging and pleading for your ex to take you back. No, stop. Remember it took both of you to get into the relationship, and if only one wants out then let him or her go.

Letting go is hard, trust me I know. If you find letting go hard to do then try some of these tips:

- Cry, cry, cry; get it out of your system.
- No one is perfect; so, get a pencil and paper and list all the things the other person did wrong in the relationship.
- Put yourself first. Think about how you want to be treated, what you want out of a relationship, and the type of partner you want in your life.
- Write all the good things you did to and for the other person in the relationship.

- Talk to someone dear to your heart about how you feel and why you feel the way you are feeling.
- Pray and ask God for strength to move on and put the pain behind you.
- After you feel you are back in control of your life, have a night out with a friend or do something special for yourself.
- Do not rush back into a relationship before you know in your heart you are over the last one.
- Do not contact your ex for a while meaning, by phone, text messaging, letters, emails, through friends, and so on. Let time heal all wounds.

Time Needed To Get Over the Relationship

You need time to get through the rough days and nights of pain. You need time to grieve, cry, feel sorry for yourself, question why, and so on. At this point, time is unlimited. Take all the time you need for yourself; but I will tell you that minutes, hours, days will not solve your problem. You need months; it even may take some years. I wouldn't advise taking years because you have a life to live and not waste. You have to let go someday but holding on for years is questionable. I would recommend counseling.

Anger

Experiencing anger during a breakup is normal. I feel once a relationship is over, I question myself...What did I do wrong? What could I have done to keep or make the relationship better? Was I the fault for the breakup? Once I answer the questions, and I realize I did all I could and didn't cause the breakup, I then become angry. I don't get even but get upset. Once I get past the anger, I then know I'm 80% over the relationship but not over him. If it was true love, it is unusual to get over the relationship in a short period. Him moving on and not wanting to work out the problems has always been my closure and knowing it's truly over. I then can move on to a new and improved relationship.

Analyze the Relationship and Problems

Take time to think about how the relationship began and the type of problems that occurred during the relationship. How often did the problems arise? Did you play a significant role in the issues? Were you both in agreement with the decision, or was it one-sided? Were you blamed for the breakup? Were both of you truly happy? This one is critical. Did you do all you could to keep the relationship healthy?

After you analyze and assess the questions, you will have many answers to the problems you had at the beginning of the breakup. This will allow you to begin to find closure. If you have unanswered questions, this is the time to contact your ex if he or she is available and wants to talk. The only thing you need to do while on the phone or in person is this:

1. Thank him or her for taking the time.

2. Tell him or her you have analyzed and assessed the relationship and you agree with the outcome but need clarification on a couple of things

3. Now, ask the questions one by one. Don't debate because you didn't ask for his or her time to argue or make things worse. You are only doing this for clarity.

4. Once you have the answers to your questions, thank him or her for taking the time and wish him or her well. You may even say "I hope we can still be friends." Expressing that there are no hard feelings. (You never know, what the future may hold.)

5. Now, you will probably cry when you end the conversation; but it's okay. These tears are tears of joy; you don't know it at this time. You are still feeling some pain after talking because you still care; plus, losing someone you loved and knowing that it is a reality and it is over is excruciating. You are at the end now, and in a few days, you will be on your way to recovery.

Forgiveness

You might find this one difficult, but I'm here to tell you that you must forgive in order to move on with your life, to find peace and closure.

By choice, you can forgive a person but never forget what you went through because remembering makes you stronger for your next relationship. You never want to make the same mistakes in a relationship, but you always want to learn from the mistakes made.

On the spiritual side, God is a forgiving God; therefore, it should not be too hard for us to forgive. Forgiving doesn't mean someone's wrong-doing is right; it just means that you forgive and hope the person understands that and has learned from the situation.

Matthew 6:14-15: **For if you forgive others their trespasses, your heavenly Father will also forgive you. But if you refuse to forgive others, your Father will not forgive our trespasses.**

Ephesians 4:31-32: **Let all bitterness and wrath and anger and clamor and slander be put away from you, along with all malice. Be kind to one another, tenderhearted, forgiving one another, as God in Christ forgave you.**

The Bible verses on forgiveness are enlightening as to

why we should forgive. Another reason is that we are all sinners, but still, we are forgiven by God.

Test Your Relationship, Take this Survey

1. Do you and your partner share secrets?
☐Yes ☐NO

2. Do you and your partner often disagree?
☐Yes ☐NO

3. Are you criticized in your relationship?
☐Yes ☐NO

4. Do you trust your partner with your life?
☐Yes ☐NO

5. Are you happy with your relationship?
☐Yes ☐NO

6. Do you kiss when you meet and leave each other?

☐Yes ☐NO

7. Do you have a date night with your partner?
☐Yes ☐NO

8. Can you talk to your partner about any problems?
☐Yes ☐NO

9. Are you sexually active with your partner enough?
☐Yes ☐NO

10. Do you tell your partner that you love them?
☐Yes ☐NO

11. Do you enjoy sex with your partner?
☐Yes ☐NO

12. Is jealousy involved in your relationship?
☐Yes ☐NO

13. If you could leave your partner, would you?
☐Yes ☐NO

14. Is your partner controlling and demanding?
☐Yes ☐NO

15. Do you find your partner funny and enjoyable?
☐Yes ☐NO

16. Is your partner your best friend?
☐Yes ☐NO

17. Do you make decisions together?
☐Yes ☐NO

18. Does your partner give you the attention you require?
☐Yes ☐NO

19. Do you feel your partner loves you?
☐Yes ☐NO

20. Would you date/marry your partner all over again?
☐Yes ☐NO

If you answered "YES" to more than ten questions, your relationship is SAFE.

If you answered "NO" to more than ten questions, your relationship is NOT SAFE.

Acknowledgments

First, I have to give Glory to God and thank him for my blessings and for giving me the opportunity, knowledge, and experience to be successful.

I want to acknowledge my best friend Willie C. Randall who came into my life, inspired and educated me to a higher standard in life.

To my daughter Starr, who is the love of my life. Who motivated and supported me along the way. Her input and encouragement allowed me to complete my book. If it weren't for her, I probably would not have finished the book.

I want to thank my siblings and parents for their support, love, and encouragement.

Thanks to all my friends, especially Dawn and Gracie, who supported me and provided their thoughts and an elegant touch of class.

Thanks to my editor, George Verongos, and to Brandon Williams for the beautiful photography.

I want to thank the women and men who participated in

my survey providing me information not only to distribute but educated me as well.

And, I would like to mostly thank those of you for purchasing, reading and supporting my book.

NOTES

NOTES

NOTES

NOTES

Made in the USA
Middletown, DE
24 June 2019